CALLANISH
THE
CROWN

First Paperback Edition 2018

Published by Angels of Light and Healing,
www.angelsoflightandhealing.org

I wish to acknowledge all dedicated researchers throughout the
centuries who have taken their time to map and study ancient
megalithic sites across Britain, also my two companions for the
journey to Callanish in 1986, and all teachers who have helped
me throughout the years. I also wish to thank my proof readers
and good friends: Lisa Rome, Isabel Parcell, Dianna Rose and
Ellen Hill, for their help and encouragement on this project.

My particular gratitude goes to Gerald and Margaret Ponting
for all their published works on Callanish. Plans of solar and
lunar alignments in this book are based on information in their
book *New Light on the Stones of Callanish* published in 1984.

The original Callanish site plan was made by Rear Admiral
Boyle T. Somerville and published in 1912.

Many thanks to everyone at the Calanais Visitor Centre for
their help, good food, and essential cups of tea which kept me
going through the storm-drenched days at Callanish in 2016.

ISBN# 978-0-9740730-5-7
Printed in Scotland

Dedicated to those who seek to understand
the timeless nature of reality...

"there is also on the island... a notable temple which is spherical in shape... the moon, as viewed from this island, appears to be but a little distance from the Earth... the god visits the island every nineteen years... the god dances continuously the night through from the vernal equinox until the rising of the Pleiades..."

Greek historian Diodorus 550 BC

CONTENTS

List of Photographs, Plans and Illustrations

To hear the stones speak requires inner silence
and a reverence for the sacred place in which you stand.

Remember this when you stand before them.

INNER VISION
THE KEY TO UNDERSTANDING

"The only real valuable thing is intuition." Einstein

While archaeologists and scientists seek to measure ancient stone circles with yardstick and sextant, I feel artists and mystics must make their understanding of these sacred places known too. For some, the idea of recording a sacred event through the eyes of the inner vision may seem to be too inaccurate to be valid. However, it is my belief that the inner sight of the artist and mystic was an integral part of the science used in the building and siting of sacred stone circles and that indeed inner vision was never considered separate from science in the way it is today.

In recent centuries we have lost our true inner vision in favor of scientific proof which often misses the intricate underlying workings of reality. As we have dissected the Earth in our quest for fragments of knowledge, we have forgotten the sublime unity of all things and the sacred, timeless energy that unites all things.

It is time for those of us who have trained our vision to see the inner worlds to speak and share our knowledge.

Though our points of reference may be different from scientists and archaeologists, we have a common bond in the search for truth. Often it is inner vision that brings profound insights to scientific inquiry. It is in this manner, I ask you to see these photographs made with technical precision, yet with the inner eye. I ask you also to think about the possibility of a truth in my words as I describe to you my inner vision at this sacred place.

Gwendolyn Awen Jones

(Opposite) Exquisite Rainbow Light at Callanish Stone Circle after Heavy Rains. June 28th 2016

CALLANISH I
THE STONEHENGE OF THE NORTH

The megalithic stone circle of Callanish I is one of the most enigmatic places on Earth dating back approximately five thousand years. Known as the *Stonehenge of the North* it is situated on the ancient Isle of Lewis.

The Isle of Lewis, surrounded by the often tumultuous storm-driven waves of the Atlantic Ocean, is one of the remote Outer Hebridean islands that lie off the North West coast of Scotland.

Though no one can ever know the true history of the people who built the Callanish I stone circle and rows, or the other smaller circles nearby, clearly they had a full understanding of the lines of force that surround the Earth. They obviously understood how the solar and lunar energies interacted with the natural energy node they chose to amplify at Callanish.

This book is written as a record of what I witnessed at Callanish when the energy node awakened to full power on the summer solstice in 1986. It is also a portrait series of each individual stone at Callanish taken on my return in 2016.

First, I will present a short history of Callanish as documented by previous scientific researchers, then I will present my own understanding of the site as witnessed through my inner vision.

(Opposite) Callanish I Stone Circle viewed from the East

PART 1

CALLANISH TIME LINE

3,000 million years ago, during the Precambrian time, the main granite rock formation of the Isle of Lewis called *Lewisian Gneiss* was formed. This is some of the oldest rock on the planet and is what was used to create the Callanish I stone circle by megalithic builders millions of years later.

3 million years ago, during the Ice Age, glaciers engulfed the land and sea around the Isles of the Outer Hebrides, Scotland and the North of England.

10,000 BC The ice melted and sea levels rose dramatically. River valleys and lower areas were flooded.

6,000 BC Over time, as the climate warmed, the area around Callanish was covered with heather moors, open grassland and small copses of hazel, silver birch and willow.

3,000 BC Pollen samples from trees and cereal crops preserved deep in the peat at Callanish indicate it was a much warmer climate than present day. Underneath the stones of Callanish there is evidence of ploughing at that time.

2,900 BC - 2,600 BC It is believed that the Callanish I Stone Circle was erected.

1,550 BC The climate began to change and became much colder.

1,150 BC Hekla volcano in Iceland erupted causing a 'nuclear' winter which would have devastated the crops. How long those freezing conditions lasted is not known but would have contributed to the cooling period that came after.

1,000 BC - 700 BC Peat began to form around the stones of Callanish. Peat only forms in damp, cool conditions. Waterlogged ground means dead plants cannot fully decay. The partially decayed matter accumulates as dense, black-brown, spongy peat. The peat slowly builds up at a rate of between half an inch and two inches in depth each hundred years.

1790 Callanish Village was settled. Villagers began cutting peat for fuel at the north end of the Callanish I megalithic site.

1857 For thousands of years the peat had accumulated reaching a depth of five feet around the main Callanish I stone circle. The peat was removed under the direction of Sir James Matheson revealing previously unrecorded smaller stones of the circle.

Clouds light up above the Silhouetted Stones of Callanish I

CALLANISH LOCATION

Low Clouds over the Outer Hebrides - Approach by Car Ferry from the Isle of Skye

Callanish is situated on the remote Isle of Lewis, which is part of the Outer Hebrides that lie off the North West coast of Scotland. The Isles of Lewis and Harris are actually one land mass but they have distinctly different terrain, Lewis tends to be flatter, more marshy with low hills, while Harris has rugged mountains. Stornoway, the main town on the island of Lewis for supplies and car rentals, can be reached by car ferry from Ullapool on the mainland of Scotland, or by air from several British mainland cities. Car ferries also dock at Tarbert on the Isle of Harris arriving from the Isle of Skye, or at Leverburgh on Harris via the Hebridean island Hopscotch ferry from North Uist.

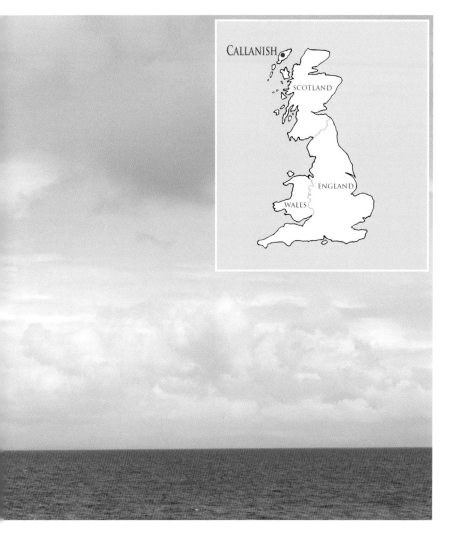

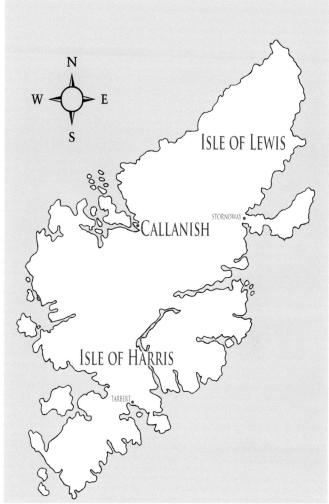

Location of Isles of Harris and Lewis in the Outer Hebrides

MEGALITHIC SITES AROUND CALLANISH

Callanish I Stone Circle on the ridge seen across the loch from Callanish II.

There are many megalithic sites in and around Callanish. Callanish I is the largest stone circle and is the main site. However, the other smaller sites are well worth a visit. The book by Gerald and Margaret Ponting *'The Stones Around Callanish'* is a good guide to these smaller sites. The map below is based on their research. The site marked as PH is on private land and requires the owner's permission to visit it. Depending on rains, some sites may require Wellington boots for safe access through marshy areas. However, the main site Callanish I is not on marshy ground and the *Calanais Visitor Centre* at that location has useful exhibitions, maps, books and hot food.

Callanish II Stone Circle

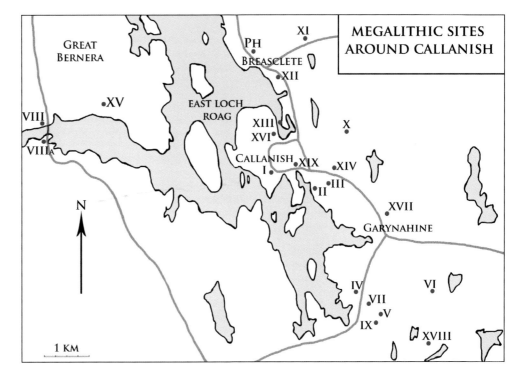

Callanish III Stone Circle

A HISTORY OF CALLANISH I STONE CIRCLE

Over 900 stone circles were built in Britain between approximately 3,400 BC and 1,350 BC.

Callanish I, situated on the island of Lewis, in the Outer Hebrides, is one of the most complete stone circles and truly impressive. Surrounded by sea lochs and cold, peat moorland hills, the circle consists of thirteen distinctly shaped stones each standing from 8 to 12 feet high. Inside the circle is the center stone towering 15' 9" in height. Leading off from the circle are five lines of stones. Two of the lines form a long corridor heading slightly east of True North. Seen from above the design of Callanish I forms a large cross with the circle at its center.

Underneath the stones of Callanish I, there is evidence of ploughing dating back to 3,000 BC. Construction of the circle was sometime between 2,900 BC - 2,600 BC. Pollen samples from trees and cereal crops preserved deep in the peat indicate that it was a much warmer climate when the stone circle was built.

Peat began to form when the climate became cooler between 1,000 BC and 700 BC. The peat eventually engulfed some of the stones completely. By 1857 when the peat was removed from the main circle, under the direction of Sir James Matheson, it had grown to a depth of five feet. Underneath the peat a burial chamber and previously unrecorded smaller stones were found. Excavations have since shown the burial cairn, which lies inside the circle, to be of a later date than the rest of the site.

The magnificent stones of the circle are of local origin and were probably brought from a quarry 1 ½ miles away. The granite used for the stone circle was formed over 3,000 million years ago and is called Lewisian Gneiss. It has veins running throughout it of white quartz, black biotite (mica) and nodules of the dark green crystal known as hornblende. The large stone known as stone #19 (shown right) at the most northerly end of the North Corridor displays the largest of these crystalline nodules of hornblende, mica and quartz.

Stone #19 with large hornblende, biotite and quartz crystal nodules.

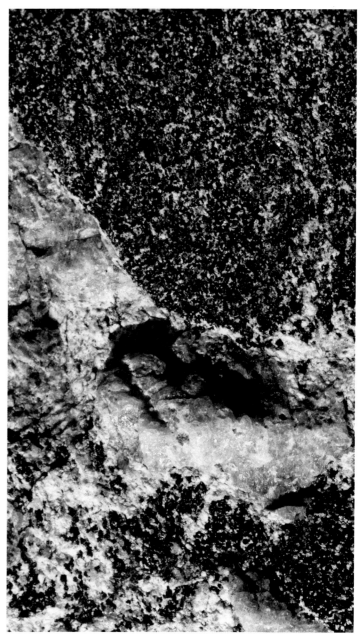

Close up of dark green hornblende, biotite and quartz crystals..

THE SOLAR CONNECTION

Antiquarians began to research Callanish I in the 1700s. Over the years that followed sketches and plans were made but they were not always accurate. In 1909 Rear Admiral Boyle T. Somerville, a naval hydrographer, made a complete survey of Callanish I. The system of numbering for the stones in this book is based upon his original plan published in 1912.

In 1933 Sir Alexander Thom, a Professor of Engineering, visited Callanish and was inspired to begin his own meticulous research into the megalithic sites of Britain detailed in his book, '*Megalithic Sites in Britain.*' He measured and decoded many stone circles in Britain and gave us key information about the sacred geometry of the ancient sites. Thom found a consistency of measure throughout these megalithic sites which he called the 'megalithic yard' measuring 2.72 feet (0.829 metres). He found that circles are often laid out in exact multiples of these megalithic yards and create precise geometrical shapes. Many of the circles, like Callanish I, were flattened on one side to a specific formula based on a code of science and mathematics very similar to the Pythagorean system. However the circle builders pre-dated Pythagoras by 1,000 years. Thom found that the circles were set out to mark astronomical events and often used 'notches' in distant mountains as key points along with complex stone alignments to chart the progress of the lunar and solar phases.

Many other researchers have added to this knowledge since Thom's work. Gerald and Margaret Ponting published '*New Light on the Stones of Callanish*' in 1984. Their research on Callanish is invaluable and highly recommended for historical details of research done to that date. In the plan opposite, using the True North/South line as my key, along with the actual drawn stone positions, I have composited Somerville's site map with important solar positions found in the Pontings' book.

While studying this overlay I noticed that the flat edge of stone number #34 indicates the general sight line for the Midsummer Sunrise if one is standing at the north edge of the central stone #29. I had often wondered why the flat edge of stone #34, an obvious notched outlier stone, was not aligned with the stones of the North Corridor. This overlay plan gave me an insight as to why. Again, standing at the north edge of the central stone #29, the Midsummer Sunset will be aligned with stone #51. When viewed from stone #29's southern edge, Midwinter Sunrise and Sunset positions will be approximately located by stones #46 and #48 respectively. The colour wheels on the plan indicate the movement of the sun for the solar extremes during the Midsummer and Midwinter Solstices and the Spring and Summer Equinoxes.

Note: this composite plan is intended to be used only as a general guide for photographers and visitors to the site for set up positions. I have not done scientific measurements at the site myself but had often wished I had a book like this before beginning my photographs for general orientation.

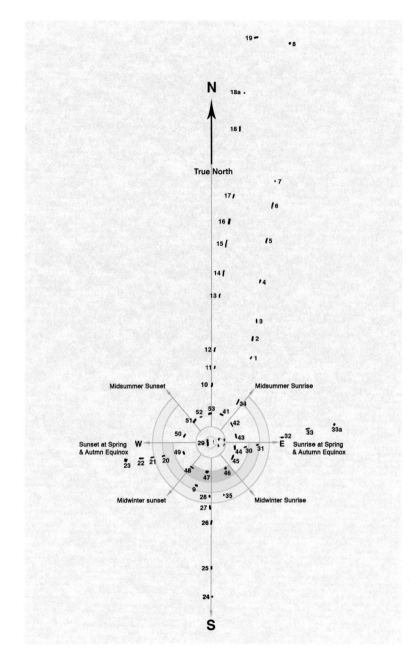

Plan of Callanish I Stone Circle with Solar Alignments

Callanish I Stone Circle Sunrise on June 22nd 1986

Moonrise seen from Callanish I Stone Circle June 21st 1986

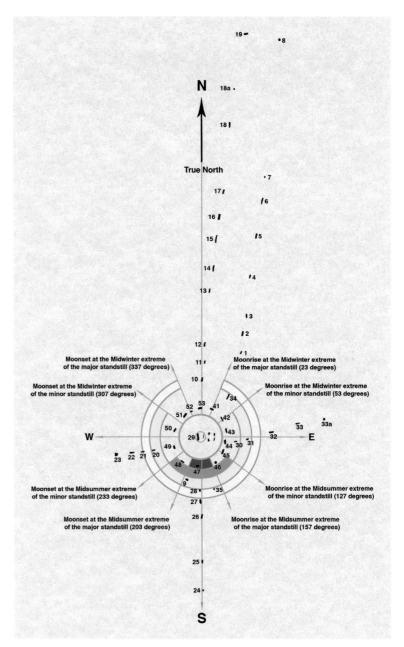

Plan of Callanish I Stone Circle with Lunar Alignments

THE LUNAR CONNECTION

"there is also on the island.. a notable temple which is... spherical in shape... the moon, as viewed from this island, appears to be but a little distance from the Earth... the god visits the island every nineteen years... the god dances continuously the night through from the vernal equinox until the rising of the Pleiades..." Diodorus 550 BC

It is most likely the Greek historian Diodorus was speaking of Lewis when he wrote the above description about the Hyperboreans in 550 BC. Due to the extreme northern latitude of Callanish, every 18.61 years a remarkable event occurs during what is known as the *Major Lunar Standstill* when the moon appears to walk across the horizon, gleaming and re-gleaming through notches in the horizon after it sets. The moon rises so close to due South that it is less than 2 degrees above the horizon. This last occurred in 1987 and 2006 and will next occur in 2025. The Major Lunar Standstill marks the turning point of a repeating pattern of lunar transits across the sky in the 18.61 year cycle. The Minor Lunar Standstill is at 9.31 years, which is the mid point of the 18.61 year cycle.

The plan opposite shows the swings of the moon's path in relation to the stones of Callanish I. The lunar extreme positions are based upon information in the Pontings' book *'New Light on the Stones of Callanish.'* I have composited that information with Somerville's original site map from the same book for this plan of lunar alignments using the True North/South line and matching the circle stones as my key. The small grey central circle on the plan marks the general position of the observer by the central stone. Viewed from the northern edge of central stone #29 the Midwinter Moonrise and Moonset locations of the Major Standstill may be found by using stones #41 and #52 respectively for orientation. Meanwhile, for the general direction of Midsummer Moonset of the Major Standstill, look south from the southern edge of stone #29 toward stone #9. For finding the position of the Midsummer Moonrise during the Major Standstill, stand at the southern edge of stone #29 and look south towards stone #35. Please be aware that this lunar plan is for general guidance to assist photographers for set up locations, I have not done measured surveys of the site myself.

The Pontings suggest that, rather than standing in the main circle itself, the most important position for viewing the moon for the Midsummer Major Lunar Standstill may be between stones #19 and #8 at the far north end of the North Corridor. Looking south from that location one can witness the moon rising out of the *'Sleeping Beauty'* range of hills and then walking across the horizon to set in the stone circle itself.

The photograph (opposite) viewed from the main circle was taken on my visit in 1986, the year before the major lunar standstill was due to occur. (I was unaware at the time of the Pontings' suggestion for viewing the moonrise.) I was lucky to see the full moon rise over the *Sleeping Beauty* range of hills on that crystal clear Midsummer night.

PART 2

THE SACRED ART OF DREAMING

"Imagination is more important than knowledge." Einstein

Since childhood I have slipped in and out of inter-dimensional doorways, seeing visions and sensing realms that others could not perceive. It was not something I often discussed as I had learned early on that these episodes were considered just my imagination by others and too strange to be real. Often I saw energies that confused me but I had no-one to explain to me what they meant. Over time I came to realize that while some people are born colour blind and others have normal sight, I on the other hand had some ability to see frequencies beyond the normal range of vision.

As a child, if I heard a note, I would perceive a colour with the sound of the note. Seeing a flashing light would create the resonant sound in my mind. I often saw into the spirit realms especially at ancient places. It was not easy having what is now termed *synesthesia* (where normally separate senses mingle e.g. sight with sound) and a super sensitivity to my surroundings. However, I learned to channel my sensitivity into art and photography.

In my early twenties I was drawn to the ancient sites of Mexico and was trained there by an old Mayan *curandera* (healer) to use my gift of sight and become a natural healer. To be a seer was a gift, she said, and I just needed to understand how to use it and not to be afraid of what I saw. She had made it plain that no drugs or alcohol should ever be used as it was important to be able to travel through the doorways of space and time and come back clean without negative energy attachments. I have always followed that advice. She also said that I must always follow my dreams and visions as it was how I would be guided throughout my life and that all work should be done for the highest good of all. After my time in Mexico I returned home to England and studied ancient sacred knowledge with healers and spiritual teachers throughout Britain and learned dowsing with the British Society of Dowsers.

Over the years, using maps and dowsing, I traced the geomagnetic energy lines, known as ley lines, across my native area of the North Yorkshire Moors and beyond. I was seeking out old stone circles, standing stones, ancient churches and places of healing. I found that most sacred sites could change the energy of the body dramatically.

We are electromagnetic beings and the Earth is one giant dynamo interacting constantly with us, the sun, planets and the cosmos. Around the Earth are pulsing magnetic lines of force. Those of us who have the sensitivity can see and feel those energy lines. Too many have lost this natural sensitivity because they are surrounded by man-made grids of electric power lines, cell towers, radio and TV transmission towers and cell phones. The Earth's ley lines still exist even so and are marked and amplified by the ancient megalithic stones circles and standing stones.

I learned to see these patterns across the landscape of Britain, and while visiting the Tor in Glastonbury, England on April 8th 1986, I was given a clear vision of the web of light radiating across the land. I saw that each ancient site had an etheric crystal above it which had a specific frequency, quite unique compared to the others. In some areas the web was shimmering with light. In others the web had become dark and the crystals either inactive or their light dimmed. I knew the crystals that had become dark were where stone circles had been damaged or destroyed. Just in the same way one can read the acupuncture meridians of the human being, so it is possible to read the Earth's own meridians. It just requires a different focus and intent to see that particular frequency.

It became clear to me that the energy pathways needed restoration for the health of the land and its people. It is well known amongst natural healers that Earth energy lines that have gone dark will cause illness in people who live in proximity to the lines. So this work was needing to be done, and soon.

The Earth itself is like a vast crystalline sphere with its own spin and sound. But she is not alone in this cosmos, there is a continual exchange of energies between her and the sun, the planets and beyond. It is a vast cosmic dance of electromagnetic energy. Any disruptions to the grid lines of the Earth throw life out of balance.

Who knows how many ancient civilizations have come and gone on this Earth or when exactly the stone circles were built? They may be far older than most suppose, perhaps connecting even to the old fabled Atlantean grid of temples now underwater.

Each crystal in the stone circle network has a specific note color and vibration. All are linked to the greater cosmic mind, and the Earth Spirit. They are part of the voice of Creation. The song of the Earth is amplified through the harmonics of the crystals that spin at the crossing nodes of the energy lines of light. At certain times of the year the power is intensified, solstices in particular are a time to note. Some circles are aligned to work with specific planetary bodies, others to star systems, all are important.

As I stood on the Tor of Glastonbury, I was shown the great circle of Callanish in the far distance on the Outer Hebrides. A vast ray entered there but the circle was out of balance, something had locked its energies. The site being the *Crown of Britain* in my vision was the most important to bring back online.

In the next weeks leading up to the solstice I had a series of dreams and intuitions about the site and how to unlock its mysteries.

THE CALL OF THE CUCKOO

Strange Dreams and Visions of Callanish

June 6th 1986

"Of whom do you speak?" Sang the cuckoo, *"We know not her words in paradise. Which woman is this that spins and dances with flames and swords of fire? She is great indeed if this is true. What kindling does she require to set this nest afire... to relinquish this body to the flames and rise as the Phoenix replenished and new? Tell her to sing more freely. Her words are but a scent in the air ... drifting, evasive. Tell her to light the fires which all will hear. Tell her to rise to her name..."*

The dream about a cuckoo calling me to Callanish left me puzzled. What did it mean to *"set the nest afire"* and what was the significance of the cuckoo at Callanish?

The next morning I was amazed to find a reference to the cuckoo mentioned in the book,*'The New Light on the Stones at Callanish'* by Gerald and Margaret Ponting. The Pontings reported that some Callanish locals held the belief, that...
"...at Midsummer sunrise the Shining One was thought to walk up the avenue of stones, heralded by a cuckoo's call...".

A shiver went down my spine as I read those words.

June 7th 1986

"The winged serpent awaits. For sun and moon spiral to-gether, blending rays of magic. A never ending dance of energy ... the twist of the serpent's tail. Moons count your days and suns your nights. The double helix spins and separates in perfect harmony within the dance of light. What deeper rays penetrate the cosmos than the sound of the one true voice rising deep from within the heart atom of each being in alignment with the truth?"

I was left wondering what any of this could mean. I just knew I was being called to be present at Callanish for some deeper purpose than I could presently understand.

June 12th 1986

I confirmed my journey to Callanish with two male companions. I had been shown I needed to work with two or four male companions to clear the site, not one or three, as a specific balance was required between male and female energies.

June 15th 1986

"The Crown will shine and become a beacon. The fires from within the center of the earth are rekindling as the sun moves to its height. The dragon awakes and begins to breathe. Restless from his sleep, his tail flicks as the energies dance to and fro. Catch the serpent as he flies and tame him. He will take you to the heart of the Earth and thence to the heart of the Eternal Void from whence all things come and return to. The serpent and the dragon are one."

June 19th, 1986

My two companions and I began our travels towards Callanish.

JOURNEY TO CALLANISH
1986

To reach the remote Isle of Lewis in the Outer Hebrides off the west coast of Scotland, my two companions and I chose to take the sea route by car ferry to the beautiful Isle of Skye, and from there to the rugged Isles of Harris and Lewis.

June 19th 1986

Taking the passage by ferry gave us a perspective of how ancient travellers would have approached these Western Isles. The sea was a rolling, steely-grey on the day we set sail from Skye. The cold salt wind stung my face as I stood on deck watching the white gulls skillfully flying in our wake against the early evening skies. Though we travelled by modern ferry, there was a sense of magic and timelessness as we sailed towards the distant island.

The long-lingering light of midsummer lit the sky with mauve and violet as we came into the harbor at the grey stone village of Tarbert. The surrounding mountains of North Harris were covered with white creeping fingers of low mist, yet above us the sky was clear. Once we had disembarked with the car we drove north through the craggy mountains of Harris, where great sea eagles still fly, towards the dark peat moorland hills and sea lochs surrounding Callanish on the west side of the Isle of Lewis.

Opposite: Mists lie heavy over mountains near Tarbert June 19th 1986

It was late evening by the time we arrived at Callanish. The tall stones stood as silhouettes against the deep indigo-blue and purple sky. There was silence.

Though the small village of Callanish lay close by, no sound disturbed the sanctity of this place. Of all the places I had seen in Britain, to me this stone circle was the crown, still whole and undisturbed by time, having been protected by peat for centuries. I felt I had reached some ancient doorway in time.

The stones, however, seemed locked by some long-forgotten magic that prevented them from speaking. To my eyes it looked as if black, gnarled, twisted energy strangled each stone, as if each was held captive by some dark force. It reminded me of how dried, blackened seaweed grips stones on the seashore, tight and suffocating.

I knew there was big work to be done to release each stone before the solstice dawn.

The waxing moon rose over the stones as we drove on our way to set camp.

Callanish I Stone Circle appeared locked by ancient magic. June 19th 1986

June 20th 1986

At 4.00 am I left my two companions asleep in the tent and climbed a hill about two miles from Callanish in order to watch the sunrise for orientation. Then, in meditation, I was given the exact information needed to clear dark web around the stones. I rejoined my companions and we reviewed the sequence of work to be done. We studied and worked with Callanish I, the main stone circle, and other smaller outlying sites II, III and IV in the Callanish complex throughout the day.

For the previous seven years, the stones had been shrouded in mist at solstice sunrise, and we were told they only showed themselves *"to those to whom it is given may see."* We could only hope that the weather would be on our side. We knew about the legend of the cuckoo heralding the arrival of the *"Shining One"* at solstice sunrise. Yet while we listened attentively for the cuckoo's song all day, expecting it to be a common sound, we heard nothing but the constant strumming wings of an acrobatic snipe as it swooped in its aerial display.

Callanish I Stone Circle viewed from within the North Corridor.

Figurative Formations in the stones of the main circle of Callanish I

We returned to the main circle of Callanish I in the evening after a full day of visits to the other smaller megalithic sites.

I was concerned when I heard a group of people drumming loudly without any kind of synchrony and not in any alignment with the natural frequency of the stones. I knew that this would hamper of the work we had come to do, which required silence, focus and pure spiritual intent. I was relieved when an old *'Keeper of the Stone*s' stormed towards them gesturing wildly. He angrily told them to leave, shouting that such noise was not in keeping with the sanctity of the place, and shooed them all away.

Silence returned as they left. The cold air smelled of the sharp tang of salt from the surrounding sea loch, mixed with the scent of damp peaty earth. I quietly made some photographs of the almost full moon over the circle and set up my camera on a tripod aligned for sunrise.

June 21st 1986

At 2.00 am after deep prayer and meditation to clear ourselves of any old patterns that might make the work impossible, and become fully connected to Source, my companions and I worked through the night with the main Callanish site by moonlight.

Using pure tones, spiritual fire, and sharp focus we broke the dark energies that had bound the site. My companions stood at each end of the row we were working on while I worked with one stone at a time, cutting and disentangling the knotted dark skeins of magic. We first worked with the stones that ran from the East to the West, then the line of stones from the South to the west side of the North Corridor, then the stones of the east side of the North Corridor back to the central circle.

Moonrise over Callanish I Stone Circle June 20th 1986

Time was short and I knew we had to complete each stone before sunrise for the circle to fully speak again.

As the solstice dawn approached, a small number of people had begun to gather at the outer stones in silence, some were setting up cameras on tripods. I knew we had to pick up speed, but with great care, as we worked to clear the stones of the central circle.

My focus was intense as I continued to unravel and cut the ancient magic that had locked the stones perhaps for thousands of years. My two companions circled the central circle in opposite directions to each other to hold the sacred space as I worked.

The cold breeze of the night had died down, and not a breath of wind stirred even the smallest grasses. A great stillness held us and yet a feeling of intense building energy was rising up around us. The stones stood sharply etched against the clear sky which was now being flushed with deep pink and orange light. It seemed to my inner sight that the stones began to flicker with an etheric rose-gold fire. The stones were beginning to 'speak' at first in a whisper, but then gradually louder as if some long, deep drum roll began to pulse from the Earth.

Then, under the ever-brightening skies, just before the sun's brilliant light came over the horizon, we completed the final release of the central stone and sang the last Oms to awaken the matrix. (Om is the Sanskrit sound of the Cosmos.)

In that very moment, to our joy, the cuckoo also began to sing, and continued to do so as the sun's shafting rays entered the circle. After a few minutes the bird fell silent and we did not hear its call again for the rest of our stay at Callanish.

(Opposite) Callanish Dawn taken the morning after Solstice June 22nd 1986

I remained at the central stone for some minutes in total awe and gratitude that we had successfully completed our work. Then I quickly sprinted back to my tripod and camera to make a photograph of the sunrise while my companions went to theirs. The morning dew had put a soft haze on the lens. I took my shot and ran back to the circle, making sure I was standing out of view of the other photographers who had gathered.

I faced the sun with my back against the central pillar. To my inner vision the circle of stones became a circle of flames and the central stone became an immense pillar of fire. The flames moved around the circle in a clockwise direction. As the intensity of the sun reached into the circle a vortex of flames began to spiral up and around the central pillar. Within the flames I saw a beautiful 'winged serpent' with alchemical body of white-gold fire bearing a gold sun upon its heart. It rose phoenix-like with blazing wings, causing what felt like great rushing winds and hissing fire to spin around me at the central stone.

The vortex reached high into the sky, meeting with what seemed to be a large, sphere of light above the circle. Each stone in the circle was over-lighted by immensely tall beings of light who were guiding the energy of the stones to the crystal sphere above the circle. Powerful arcs of light went between each of the stones in the circle to the sphere above. The sphere above looked like a beautiful multi-faceted crystal and was much larger in circumference than the stone circle below. As it became more highly charged it glowed with the light of a thousand suns and it too began to spin slowly clockwise. As it radiated light and energy across the land I heard a wonderful deep sound within my being as if all Creation sang. The feeling was indescribable, one of cosmic alignment with the Source. Pure joy and elation!

Though there were several people at the site, most were focused on getting the sunrise onto film. No one else seemed to see what I was seeing, not even my two companions though they had felt changes in the energy around us and shifts within themselves, they had no inner vision to see what I told them I was witnessing. However, a short while later a stranger to our group, a young woman, spoke independently to one of my companions and told him that she too had seen a vision of a phoenix-like figure of fire rising from the circle of flames at sunrise. My companion was amazed to hear that confirmation.

All morning long the brilliance from the crystal shone out across the Isle of Lewis re-energizing the land. Then, at around 3.00 pm, when the sun was at its height, the energy of the circle seemed to reach a peak and powerful shafts of light shot out with a great sound from the glowing crystal orb above, like so many golden arrows flying all across the land. I saw sacred sites throughout Britain light up like beacons in response.

(Opposite) Callanish I Stone Circle a few minutes after Solstice Sunrise at 4.24 am June 21st 1986

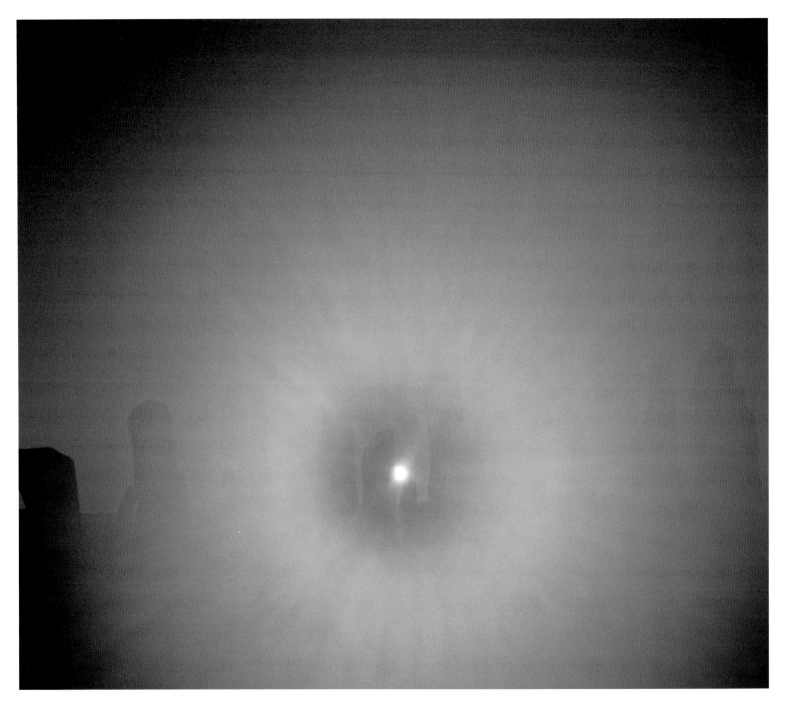

Later that day I made a sketch of the stones in pen and ink and tried to depict the solar crystalline sphere above, but I found the faceted structure too complex to draw. Depicting energies from inter dimensional worlds beyond normal physical sight is difficult because there are no hard and fast edges to define them. The sheer brilliance of the crystal energy made it hard to look at directly. I could not tell if the facets were five or six sided, or something else, but I wanted to make a record as I knew I would not be able to photograph this aspect of what was happening at Callanish.

Years later I enhanced my original sketch in Photoshop to depict the glow of the solar sphere. (See below.)

Pen & Ink Sketch of Callanish I Stone Circle with the Solar Crystalline Sphere Above. June 21st 1986

Solstice Moonrise begins over Cnoc an Tursa from Callanish I Stone Circle June 21st 1986

That evening, just after sunset, I watched from inside the circle as the full moon rose over the mound of Cnoc an Tursa to the south. The stones began to resonate again but this time it was the moon activating them and a definite etheric blue flame hovered around each stone. I wished I could have captured that luminescence on film. As it was, I struggled to capture the moment on my 25 ASA Kodachrome film due to limited light, which meant for a very a shallow depth of field.

Solstice Moonrise from Callanish I Stone Circle June 21st 1986

After a few shots I climbed the mound of Cnoc an Tursa to watch the events unfold from a higher vantage point.

A beautiful silver-blue vortex of light began to spin anti-clockwise around the stones. This vortex was focussed downwards and charged up a large blue energy sphere deep in the Earth below the circle. This lunar sphere had its own unique sound quite different to the solar sphere, but exquisitely beautiful. The lunar sphere then began to slowly spin in an anti-clockwise direction while the solar sphere maintained its own clockwise spin above. In the long twilight hours I watched an amazing exchange of light dance between the solar and lunar energy fields conducted through the harness of the central stone of the circle. As they intertwined, I saw that they created the double helix form of the DNA. I watched in awe as a massive toroidal field was generated through and around the circle. Whoever built this circle knew exactly what they were creating: the basic structures of life!

The massive circuitry of the Callanish I stone circle and outlying rows seemed linked via the crystals in the stones in such a way to draw the Earth's lines of force into a divine harmony with the solar and lunar spheres. The stones with their large dark-green crystalline nodules of hornblende, black mica and white quartz crystals must have been specifically chosen for their ability to conduct Earth, solar, lunar and cosmic energies to vitalize the land.

My body felt powerfully charged and energized. I felt more alive than ever, my mind and inner vision seemed crystal clear and I was seeing beyond the physical stones as if I had passed through the doorway in time.

I felt no need for sleep.

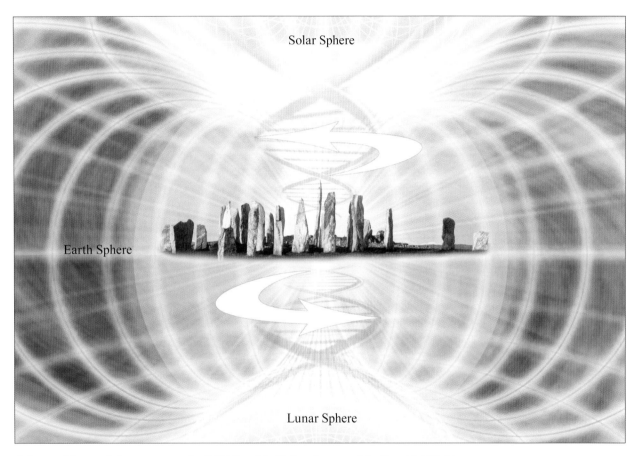

Solar and Lunar Spheres create the DNA Double Helix - Image of the Toroidal Fields
It was almost impossible to describe the exquisite beauty of the solar and lunar spheres as they turned in opposite directions to create the DNA double helix. Years later I attempted to create an image of the toroidal fields but this schematic cannot truly show the beauty of what I saw.

Solstice Night Moonrise over the 'Sleeping Beauty' hills and the loch at Callanish June 21st 1986

As the moon rose higher over the stones and shimmered across the loch, I returned to the camp and watched the night through. As my companions slept, I stayed alone in deep silence and prayer and I watched as the phoenix took form again in the flames of the campfire.

My mind reached out through time. Ancient memories were stirred by the flickering dance of fire across the glowing embers. I knew I had been here before... a long, long time ago...

4.23 am June 22nd 1986 Sunrise at Callanish I, first glimmer of light through the stones

June 22nd 1986

My companions continued to sleep as the first traces of light touched the early morning sky. Though I was tired I wanted to make photographs to record the stones in the short time we had before we had to leave.

At 3.30 am I returned alone to the stone circle to make photographs of the dawn and sunrise. A small group of people had also returned, but left shortly after the sun had risen at 4.21 am.

SPIRIT STONES

After 4.30 am I was alone at the stones. The real events of the solstice as I had seen them had seemed impossible to capture on film, but as I started to make my photographs within the stillness of those early hours, the stones became alive again to my sight.

During the solstice sunrise I had witnessed seeing immensely tall beings of light, at least twice the size of the stones in the circle, each being over-lighting a specific stone. Were these beings the ancient *Spiritual Guardians* of the place? I did not know. But they knew how the energy worked and how to guide it.

The central pillar was the conduit stone, which I had been standing against during the solstice. I do not remember a being over-lighting that particular stone, but it became the focus of all the energy in the circle.

Other than the central stone, the stone with which I'd had the strongest spiritual link to during the solstice sunrise was stone #45. This stone's natural markings, which I had photographed the day before, reminded me of a pictograph of a human figure similar to ones I had seen in other ancient cultures.

Alone in the early morning light I quietly made photographs using 25 ASA Kodachrome colour film and 400 ASA black and white film to record the textures of the stones. (In 1986 digital cameras were not available and every shot on film had to count.) A tripod allowed for a slow meditative pace.

(Opposite page) Sunrise shafts through the stones of Callanish I 4.26 am June 22nd 1986

(Above) Ancient Figure in the crystal patterns of stone #45 June 20th 1986

Spirit Shadow 1. Long shot of Shadow on Stone #45   *Spirit Shadow 2. Medium shot of Shadow on Stone #45*

I had been working along the North Corridor of stones and as I made my way back towards the stone circle, there was a tangible static charge in the air and a feeling of hushed excitement as if I was about to walk into another realm.

While walking around the circle I saw the shadow of a figure on the back of stone #45 that I had not noticed before. The torso, I could see was most likely cast by another stone, but the head and headdress...? I could not see what could have made it as the stone appeared from my view point to have a fairly smooth surface with no deep indentations. I took one photograph on my old Rolleicord camera and wound on the film.

I approached closer, and again felt that deep heart connection similar to the day before, as if for one brief moment the *Spirit Guardian* who had over-lighted that particular stone was giving me a chance to photograph the impossible. Was it just a trick of the light or an encounter with one of the *Guardians* of the stones? I made another photograph half expecting the shadow to disappear or not show on the film. Then, holding my breath, I stepped closer yet and made one last shot. (See over page.)

(Opposite page) Early Morning Light looking north along the west side of the North Corridor of stones June 22nd 1986

Spirit Shadow 3. Close up of Shadow on Stone #45

The mystery of the spirit shadow remained with me for thirty years until I returned to Callanish again in 2016. On the morning of June 20th 2016, at 5.54 am, I was able to capture the image of the spirit shadow once more as it suddenly appeared when the sun momentarily pierced through the heavy clouds.

On closer inspection I saw there were shallow indentations in the surface just deep enough to create the shadow for the head and headdress of the figure. Was the stone intentionally carved that way as a hidden portrait of one of the original builders of the site, or is it just a natural feature eroded into the stone by tumultuous storms throughout the aeons of time? Whether by chance or by design, the full form of the spirit shadow can only be seen when the sun is at a certain angle to stone #45 at that very early hour.

(Opposite) The Spirit Shadow Reappears 5.54 am June 20th 2016

June 22nd 1986

7.00 am. After being awake for so many hours I finally felt a need for sleep and returned to camp. I woke again at noon, my face on fire with the sun. My companions were just waking also. We returned to the stones together and sat within the circle to meditate and sang Oms again to reconnect to the central stone. The crystal above expanded through our hearts, and, through its thousands of facets, sent light around the globe connecting with all the great etheric crystals centered at sacred sites around the Earth. The two spirals of energy from the crystals above and below the site merged with the sphere around the circle of stones into one great sphere of light around us.

The three spheres became one.

A beautiful light surrounded each one of us. We three hugged together and smiled. None of it had been easy. We had each faced personal challenges along the way and had to face our inner shadows in one way or another. I was so grateful that we were able to accomplish the work.

Many years later I would learn that Callanish I, which I have called *The Crown of Britain,* is considered to be a major node on the Earth's grid. The grid consists of a matrix of powerful lines of energy that flow around the Earth. Nodes are where the energy lines cross each other and interact. (See *'Earth Grids'* by Hugh Newman published in 2008.) I believe that Callanish I acts as a conduit for life-giving energy. It links with the other major nodes on the Earth's grid, and, together, they maintain the well-being of the body of the Earth, and the health of those living upon it.

June 23rd 1986

It was time to leave Callanish but the memories would remain etched in my consciousness forever. I knew I would never forget all I had witnessed but also kept copious notes for what would become this book. I felt it was important not to publish the information at that time to protect the sanctity of the site. Now the story of the my understanding of the stones should be told for those who will come after me.

I remain deeply grateful to my two companions, the old *Keeper of the Stones* and the *Spirit Guardians* from the other realms who came to assist us, without whom the work could not have been achieved.

Before leaving the area we took a short journey south to the Isle of Harris and ran along the white sand beach there, plunging into the ice cold sea to refresh ourselves. From there we visited the area where sea eagles are known to fly. Then returning north again we headed to Stornoway to be ready for the early ferry the next morning.

June 24th 1986

While on the ferry to Ullapool I stood alone on deck to complete the work with the great crystal above Callanish. It was an immense light above the Isle of Lewis and a beautiful light in my heart as I quietly sang. I knew this journey could never be repeated in the same way. The work was done.

Within a few days my companions and I had gone our separate ways. Bidding each other farewell.

Sunset on the Road to Stornoway June 23rd 1986

June 28th 1986

London. I was taking a workshop by the well-known researcher Keith Critchlow who was describing the ancient teachings of time, space and sacred geometry. I shared with Keith all I had witnessed at Callanish; that the stones seemed to create, charge up and enhance the DNA.

Keith was not surprised by my description or about the great crystal-like energy spheres above and below the site on the inner plane creating the DNA double helix pattern through the central stone. Having surveyed many sacred sites himself, described in great detail in his book *'Time Stands Still'* (published in 1982), Keith simply smiled and said, "Of course!"

PART 3

RETURN TO CALLANISH
2016

After thirty years of travel as a healer and photographer I decided to revisit Callanish again to reconnect with the site and complete the work of recording the stones that I had begun in 1986. I had often wondered if the stones had remained energetically clear since the work done years ago.

June 16th 2016

I flew to Stornoway on the Isle of Lewis, rented a car and took a room at a local bed and breakfast not far from Callanish. I knew this would not be a camping trip and was glad it was not as the weather began to turn for the worse. It was my desire this visit to make a portrait of each stone and show its location within the circle. So I began work in earnest with only a few days to complete the photographs for this book.

I was glad to see that the new *Calanais Visitor Centre* was carefully hidden below the view of the stones to the South, and it became a welcome place to retreat to during the heavy rain storms for warm food, information and books. Over the next few days, the rains came and went, punctuated by brief spells of sunshine. Buses disgorged tourists at regular intervals and folks tended to get in the way of wide shots while they were taking selfies, but they would soon disappear as fast as they had come just like the passing rain clouds, moving on to the next venue. Camper vans unfortunately marred the view of the stones at the north end and none of the travellers were keen to briefly move their vehicles as they were firmly encamped for the coming solstice.

I found that early mornings and late evenings were the best time for photography with fewer crowds, although there were always a few solstice travellers gathered for each expected sunrise and sunset at the circle who had their own ways of connecting with the stones. As dark clouds obscured each sunrise and sunset I began to think of the old saying that the stones only showed themselves *"to those to whom it is given may see."*

(Opposite) Callanish I Stone Circle with stones #42 and #41 in foreground

Callanish I Stone Circle with the Mound of Cnoc an Tursa viewed from the east looking west

The mound of Cnoc an Tursa is seen to the left of the picture above. It is a major part of the circuitry of the main Callanish I site and links directly through the stones of the South Row to the central stone #29. I am not sure if the mound has ever been excavated but I do know it is a major energy portal for the site's operation. More megalithic structures may lie beneath the mound.

Callanish I Stone Circle seen from the East Row looking west

The photograph above viewed from the East of the Callanish I stone circle is in the same general orientation as the image on the preceding page. The foreground stone is #32 of the East Row. The tallest central stone #29 in the middle, is angled upwards.

A Break in the Storm Clouds over the loch at Callanish.

Very early each morning I would return to the stones before sunrise, often watching as storms raged across the area. Perhaps it was the rain, or the travellers and their strange rituals, or too many tourists each day, but it seemed as if a grey confused energy had descended around the stones, their inner light was hidden to my sight. No *Keeper of the Stones* came to command silence this time. Perhaps he had long since passed? I began to realize what remarkable good fortune I'd had 30 years ago to witness the solstice sunrise in the way I had.

One morning I was in conversation with a lady whose house sits close to the stone circle. I admired the pretty flowers in her garden and commented that I had not seen many flowers in Callanish. She said that the weather, wind and sheep made it hard to grow much in the area, but her walled garden was sheltered and kept the sheep out.

The night before had been a particularly drenching storm so I said in agreement about the weather, *"We had quite a heavy rain storm last night."*

She looked up from the flowers she was tending to and smiled, *"Oh no dear, that wasn't a heavy rain, that was just damp!"*

Interested in her idea of *"just damp",* as I had been soaked to the skin even in my rain gear the night before, I asked what was the weather like in winter.

"Oh!" She said with a deep sigh, *"Terrible storms! 100 mph wind and rain that comes parallel to the ground!"*

Early Morning Callanish I Stone Circle after a storm 5.51 am June 19th 2016

June 20th 2016
Another stormy morning. Sunrise should have been at 4.21 am but was totally obscured by clouds again.

The sun briefly broke through the clouds at 5.58 am and lit up the central stone from behind with solar 'fire' in a most spectacular way. It was as if the stones were trying to wake up from the gloom. (See photo on next page.)

Solar 'Fire' lights up the central stone during a stormy morning at Callanish 5.58 am June 20th 2016

Solstice Dawn under Leaden Skies at 3.50 am June 21st 2016 Callanish I viewed from the west looking east.

June 21st 2016

3.45 am. I got to the stones very early in hope of seeing the solstice sunrise at 4.21 am. It was raining again. Would the sun break through? I waited with my camera and tripod outside the circle while the solstice travellers partook of their rituals by the central stone.

The specified time for sunrise arrived and the sun did not appear. Not even a glimmer. No cuckoo called and the stones remained strangely quiet and brooding under the leaden skies. There was a heaviness in the air and I thought again of the saying, *"to those to whom it is given may see..."* as the rain-soaked travellers slowly drifted away.

I continued to make portraits of the stones each day, however I was not able to complete the whole set of the stones as I had intended without camper vans being in the view and my flight back to Edinburgh came all too soon. Locals explained that it was best to visit the stones at other times of the year and suggested that in just one week most of the solstice travellers would be gone. I took note and decided to return about a week later.

Solstice Dawn at 4.08 am June 21st 2016 Callanish I Stone Circle viewed from the north looking south toward the mound of Cnoc an Tursa. (Heavy clouds obscured Solstice Sunrise at 4.21 am.)

June 22nd 2016

I flew from Stornoway back to Edinburgh and after a few days there I decided to visit other parts of Scotland before returning to the Isle of Lewis by ferry. I was hoping for a clearer view of the stones on my return.

Following the paths of my ancestors to Rothes where my great, great grandmother had lived in a crofter's cottage, I continued my way via Inverness to Ullapool to overnight there in a small B&B, ready for the early morning ferry back to the Isle of Lewis.

June 28th 2016

On the ferry I had to smile when I overheard a sodden tourist say, while looking out across a dark sea through the rain squalls, that she was wishing summer would come. Her companion replied, *" But honey this* is *summer!"*

Back Road to Callanish in heavy rain.

On my return to Callanish I finally got the last shots I needed while still dodging heavy rains storms and the occasional soaked tourists. One week past the solstice most of the crowds had indeed gone and only one camper van remained discreetly out of view.

For the shot below I had waited in my car for well over an hour for the storm to pass and not a soul was in sight as the rain pummelled the car. Then, just as a sudden break in the clouds allowed for a double rainbow to show, a television film crew sped up the hill in a large van with cars following. The crew leapt out and said they needed to film, asked me to stand back and promptly took over the site with their crew and a drone. Misty rain kept spattering on my lens as I waited for them to be out of the way of my shots. The film crew left after the best of the light but I stayed and quietly made other shots. At 10.38 pm as the sun set, a rich orange, pink and purple light lit the heavy clouds from below. It was worth the wait. (See next spread over page.)

Double Rainbow after hours of heavy rain just before Sunset 10.17 pm June 28th 2016. (Sunset was at 10.35 pm that night.)

Stormy Last Light at Callanish I viewed from the east side of the circle 10.38 pm June 28th 2016

Rainbow over Callanish I 9.39 pm June 29th 2016

June 29th 2016

It was a quieter time at the site. Very few tourists, no film crews and no solstice travellers. It seemed as if the Callanish stones relaxed in the silence.

I had been hoping for another chance of a rainbow at Callanish. With all the storms passing through I kept an eye on the light throughout the day. Though it was not a double rainbow, like the night before, a single rainbow formed above the stones and I was grateful to see it and made my shot. (See opposite page.)

Earlier in the evening I had been driving back towards Callanish when I saw a peculiar rainbow with three arcs, but not all aligned. A most unusual sight. (See photograph below.) I can only surmise that the clouds must have somehow separated shafts of light, each shaft creating its own rainbow.

Triple Rainbow with an unusual alignment.

Beautiful Evening Skies at Callanish I looking east 10.08 pm June 29th 2016

There were only two others at the stones on the evening of the 29th June. One man in his 40's who seemed to understand the stones, and another man, much older, who was peacefully standing at the end of the East Row as if he was drawn to be a part of a sacred communion with them.

The younger man went quietly to the end of the West Row and sat with his dog looking out towards the setting sun which was just peeking out under the heavy clouds. This was the same configuration of energy I'd had when I worked with my two companions in 1986, the male energy acting as a ground for the female energy within the circle.

I was finally able to go into the circle without the distractions of tourists and stood with my back against the central stone. After a silent prayer to clear the confused energies from the site and a tone to awaken the stones, the stones began to speak again. Not as loud as 30 years ago, nor did they carry the solar fire as this was not the solstice sunrise. The sun had now set and rain clouds still hung heavy above obscuring any moon that might have been rising, but I was glad to feel the divine grace once more in my body as the energy moved up the central stone.

We three stayed in silent communion with the stones until 11 pm. Then, I stepped out of the circle and turned to the East, and with a gentle wave of my hand in recognition of his part, I smiled in the direction of the older man. He gave a stately nod in acknowledgement and left without a word, a soft spiritual light hovered around his body in the dim light as he walked away. Was he the old *Keeper of the Stones* who had returned, or another? I was not sure. Whoever he was he knew how to hold the sacred energy of the place.

The younger man and I walked towards each other in silence. Then like old spiritual travellers on converging paths for that moment in time we talked of sacred work and ancient sites we knew across Britain. Gradually the cold, damp night air got deep into my bones and he offered to brew tea in his camper. We sipped the hot tea in mugs outside looking towards the great circle and talked till 11.45 pm.

"To hear the stones speak," I said, *"requires inner silence and a reverence for the sacred place in which you stand."*

He agreed and said very few people understood. In deep gratitude we bade each other farewell and safe travels. I never did get his name, he said he preferred to be unknown. It is often the way of spiritual workers who come to an inner call.

Callanish I viewed from the east early morning

PART 4

PORTRAITS OF THE STONES

The plan I have used throughout this book of Callanish I Stone Circle has the numbering first published by Somerville in 1912. I have to admit I found his system quite baffling as I made my photographs of the site, but have followed it as other publishers have used this sequence and I do not want to cause any further confusion. So to keep things relatively sane I have broken the site down into sections.

In some of the photographs I have reversed the numerical sequence of the photographs to match the actual visual sequence as I walked down the row or corridor in order to better show the flow of energy from one stone to the next. So don't let the numbering confuse you. Just read the stones in relation to each other as you would a musical score. Each sequence of stones is highlighted on the plan with that particular page spread.

1. Stones of the South Row.
2. Stones offset from Rows.
3. Stones of the West Row.
4. Stones of the East Row.
5. Stones of the North Corridor, West Side.
6. Stones of the North Corridor, East Side.
7. Stones of the Main Circle.
8. Stones of the Cairn.

Callanish I viewed from the north-east early morning.

STONES OF THE SOUTH ROW

Walking up the path from the Visitor Center by the mound of Cnoc an Tursa the first stones encountered are those of the South Row which lead to the main circle of Callanish I. Stone #24 is the first stone in the South Row and seems not to be a powerful node but is a receiving stone. The mound of Cnoc an Tursa, however seems to be a strong node point and acts as a transmitter of energy to the site through stone #24. I do not know if Cnoc an Tursa has ever been excavated to reveal what stones lie beneath it but I do know a lot of energy enters at that point and it is a major part of the circuit for the site. Each stone shapes the Earth's energy as it flows through and around it. I think of the stones as a series of deliberately shaped 'instruments' and just like tuning forks they resonate at very specific frequencies. Together they modulate the frequencies and create a perfect harmony. When activated by the sun and moon on specific days such as the summer and winter solstices they begin to 'sing.'

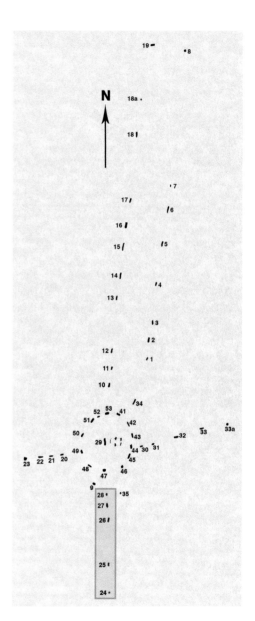

It is very possible the stones harness the solar and lunar energies at other times of the year and also resonate with the energies of galactic influences. I have not spent enough time with them to know. What I do know is that it is best to attune to the stones in silence. Take your time to quiet your mind so that you may experience each stone's energy.

STONES OFFSET FROM ROWS

There are three stones that are offset, which, at first sight, do not belong to any row or the main circle (shown opposite). They most likely mark important line-up positions for solar or lunar events. Stone #9 and # 35 stand either side of the South Row and outside of the main circle. Stone # 34 stands outside the circle on the opposite side of the circle to stone #9.

As I merged the overlay map of solar alignments onto the main plan of the circle, stone #34 seemed to have a general line up for the Midsummer Sunrise if viewed from the central stone of the circle # 29.

Stone #9, if viewed from the southern edge of the center stone #29, indicates the general position of moonset at the Midsummer Extreme of the Major Lunar Standstill. The broken stone number #35 is known to have been repaired in Victorian times. I think it was originally placed by the circle builders to mark the position of the moonrise at the Midsummer Extreme of the Major Lunar Standstill. When #35 is viewed from the southern edge of stone #29 it may be used for a general line-up for that lunar event for photographers.

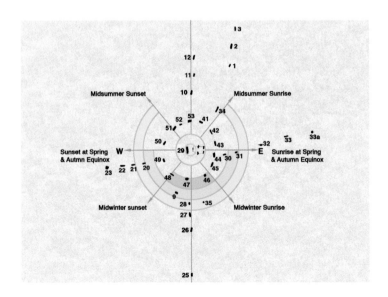

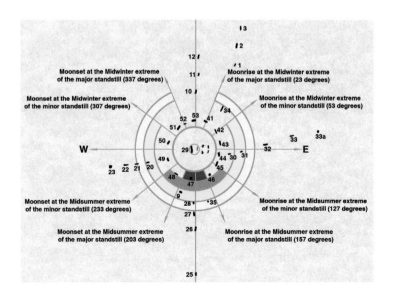

STONES OFFSET FROM ROWS

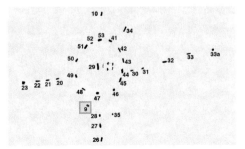

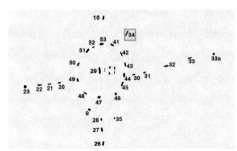

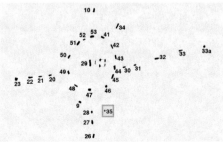

STONES OF THE EAST ROW

Although this sequence appears numerically backwards, I have shown the East Row in correct sequence as it is viewed from the north looking south. Each stone at Callanish has tremendous character and is unique. Some seem to have figures of otherworldly beings in the natural blends of crystals, others have very linear patterns.

The shape and size of each stone seems to be specific for that location within the site. Nothing is random. This is a remarkable achievement by the original builders to harness the Earth energies. The stones are definitely planned for lunar and solar work and also perhaps for interplanetary alignments. Taking the time in silence to feel the outer energy of each stone either with the hands or with dowsing rods shows the extent of the fields generated by each stone. There are definite electromagnetic energy fields linking the stones.

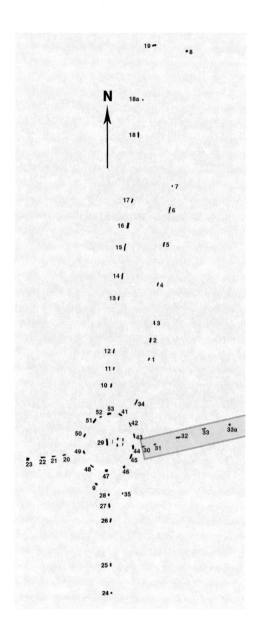

Unfortunately there are places where stones appear to be missing in the site. A map made by J.L.Palmer in 1857 showed the existence of stone 33a however the stone had fallen and become buried below the turf for over 100 years. It was found at the end of the East Row by Gerald and Margaret Ponting in 1977 and it was re-erected in its original post hole which luckily had also been located in July 1982.

Stone #33a is a powerful node stone, which harnesses and grounds energy, and seems to link to distant sites Callanish II and Callanish III that lie across the loch to the East.

STONES OF THE WEST ROW

The north faces of the West Row of stones are shown here. The mound of Cnoc an Tursa can be seen to the South behind them. Notice the large hornblende nodules on stone # 22. The stones have broad faces but tend to be narrow from the side view.

Stone #23 (opposite page) at the end of the West Row has a slightly squarer base and acts as a blocking stone *and* a node stone. A blocking stone corrals the energy within the circuit and directs the flow back into the site, and, at the same time, blocks any other energies from entering the circuit that would not be appropriate for the designed resonance of the site. Equinox sunrise approximate position can be located from this stone by looking along the West Row through the circle. To find the Equinox sunset approximate position stand in the main circle while looking along the West Row towards stone #23.

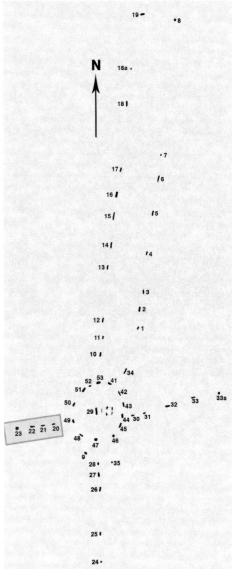

STONES OF THE NORTH CORRIDOR (WEST SIDE)

Stones #10 - #19 are pictured here as viewed from inside the North Corridor in the sequence seen while walking north away from the main circle. The east faces of the stones are shown here. There are gaps in this line suggesting there are stones missing. #18a on the plan marks the

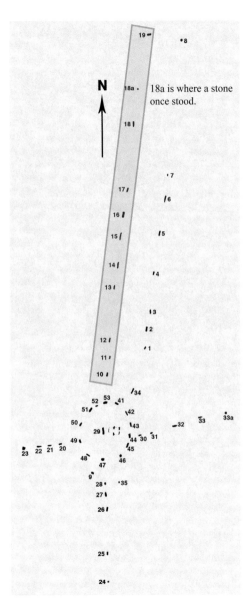

18a is where a stone once stood.

position of one missing stone. Stone #19 (pictured with stone #8 behind it) is viewed from the northwest to show its large hornblende nodules. #19 is a powerful node stone at the end of the North Corridor. One of my favourite stones for personality has to be #11 (close-up shown above).

STONES OF THE NORTH CORRIDOR (EAST SIDE)

The east side of the North Corridor begins with node stone #8 at the far north end. Stones #8 - #1 are viewed here in sequence as seen while walking inside the corridor back towards the main circle. The west faces of the stones are shown here.

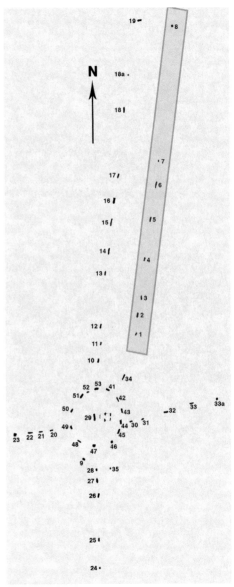

Stone #4 close up (shown above.) This stone has definite personality. Like a pensive gnome, he looks north away from the main circle along the line of stones and the tip of his 'hat' points back towards the circle.

STONES OF THE MAIN CIRCLE

The stones of the main circle are part of a massive generating system that seems to accelerate the electromagnetic potential of the Earth. During the Midsummer Solstice sunrise of June 21st 1986 the stones began to charge up with energy. That energy began to slowly flow around the circle in a clock-

wise spiral, gathering speed. It then went up and around the central stone towards a large sphere of light above. That same evening, as the full moon rose, the lunar energies flowed in an anti-clockwise spiral around the circle, then to the central stone and downwards to a large sphere of energy below the site.

STONES OF THE MAIN CIRCLE

Each large stone of the main circle has a distinct personality. Some have almost human like shapes, so one can understand old folk tales of giants being turned to stone here. Perhaps those 'giants' were the same tall *Spiritual Guardians* I witnessed in 1986? They came for the Midsummer

Solstice and were conducting the energy flows to the large sphere above the circle to enhance the life energy of the Earth. However one looks at these stones they are beautiful in their own right. Treat them with great respect and you may see what is beyond the physical realm.

STONES OF THE MAIN CIRCLE

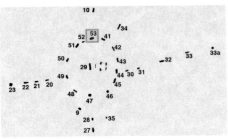

Stone #29 is the central megalith. It is 15' 9" tall and weighs about 5-6 tons. It is a thin slab with its widest faces oriented East/West. The linear set of the stone is approximately aligned North/South. The top edge is angled upwards in the direction of north and acts an easy reference point for orientation while at the site.

This central stone is the receiver for all the energies coming into the circle. From my experience at the site it is the pivotal point through which the solar and lunar vortices interact. The main circle stones and all the outlying stones are a massive circuit. Stone #29 at the center acts as the still point within the toroidal field generated.

The east face of stone #29 (shown left) has nodules of the dark green hornblende crystals, mixed with black mica and white quartz.

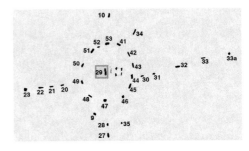

Stone #53 is a receiving stone for the North Corridor's incoming energies.

CAIRN STONES WITHIN THE CIRCLE

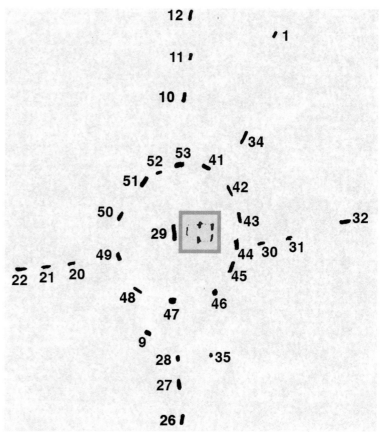

Cairn stones 36, 37, 38, 39, 40 and 41a shown inside box above are found within the main circle. The entry way is between circle stones 43 and 44 facing east aligned the Spring and Autumn Equinox Sunrise.

The chambered cairn was excavated in 1857 and found to have the remains of a cremation within it. The cairn was added much later to circle so it should not be considered to be part of the orignal solar/lunar site design.

9.57 pm June 30th 2016 Light shafts through Callanish I as the sun begins to set. Sunset that day was due at 10.34 pm.

June 30th 2016

The heavy rains continued on and off during my last night at the stones. Rain squalls came through abruptly changing the light and patterns on the landscape.

At 9.57 pm the sun broke through the clouds for a few moments and a shaft of gold light lit the center of the Callanish stones. (See opposite page.)

Just 2 minutes later at 9.59 pm everything changed as gusting winds brought more heavy rain. The ensuing torrent obliterated the sun. (See photograph on next pages 86-87.)

Undaunted, I waited to see if the sun would give me one last blaze of glory. Sunset was due at 10.34 pm but the clouds did not part as they continued their wild dance across the sky. No sunset brilliance came to end the day – just misty rain.

By 10.39 pm the rain had stopped and all that remained were the black silhouettes of the stones against a deep blue sky. The menacing clouds had retreated low into the distant horizon leaving just one single streak of pink catching the last light. (See photograph on pages 88-89.)

I had done what I had set out to do and I knew it was time to leave the stones of Callanish. Packing up my camera and tripod I stopped for a moment, gave thanks to the great *Spirit Guardians* of this place and to the *Keeper of the Stones,* whoever he was, and sang one last tone to the stones. Then I turned towards the car not knowing if I would ever return to Callanish. Would I be called again?

July 1st 2016

I headed south to Tarbert to explore the beautiful rugged Isle of Harris for two days before heading back to the mainland. Rains continued on and off.

July 3rd

From Leverburgh on the Isle of Harris I took the ferry to North Uist and then to the Isle of Skye. The sea was as black as liquid tar with white foam crests under intense storm clouds as we sailed. Above the low rumble of the ferry's engines and the sound of the waves breaking around the bow, in my mind I was hearing my mother sweetly singing *"Over the sea to Skye..."* Old childhood memories. I smiled. Was it something in her ancient blood line that had called me back?

The Isle of Skye was shrouded in misty rain as the ferry came into the harbour. On disembarking, there was no need to linger. I headed back to the mainland and onto the next assignment.

9.59 pm June 30th 2016 Misty rain obscures the sun at Callanish I. Sunset was due at 10.34 pm.

Dusk at Callanish 10.39 pm June 30th 2016

Bibliography

New Light on the Stones of Callanish by Gerald and Margaret Ponting published 1984

The Stones around Callanish by Gerald and Margaret Ponting published 1984

Callanish & Other Megalithic Sites of the Outer Hebrides by Gerald Ponting published 2002

Megalithic Sites in Britain by A.Thom published 1967

Megalithic Lunar Observatories by A. Thom published 1971

Megalithic Remains in Britain and Brittany by A.Thom and A.S. Thom published 1978

Time Stands Still by Keith Critchlow published 1982

A Guide to Ancient Sites in Britain by Janet & Colin Bord published 1979

The New View over Atlantis by John Michell published 1969

A Little History of Astro-archeology by John Michell published 1977

Megalithomania by John Michell published 1982

The Old Straight Track by Alfred Watkins published 1925

The Sun and the Serpent by Hamish Miller & Paul Broadhurst published 1989

Earth Grids by Hugh Newman published 2008

Maps of the Ancient Sea Kings by Charles H. Hapgood published 1986

Megalith: Studies in Stone by Hugh Newman published 2018

Stone Circles by Hugh Newman published 2017

For books, maps and information about Callanish contact **Calanais Visitor Centre** www.callanishvisitorcentre.co.uk

Stone wall and green fields on the Isle of Lewis with a view to the Atlantic Ocean

INDEX OF STONES BY NUMBER

1-8 Stones of the North Corridor (East Side)
9, 34, 35 Stones Offset from Rows
10-19 Stones of the North Corridor (West Side)
20-23 Stones of the West Row
24-28 Stones of the South Row

29 Central Megalith
30-33a Stones of the East Row
36-41a Cairn Stones inside the Main Circle
41-53 Stones of the Main Circle

Stone #32 of the East Row June 19th 2016

ABOUT THE AUTHOR

Gwendolyn Awen Jones is an award winning author known for her books on healing and spirituality. She was born with a natural gift of spiritual sight that allows her to see the subtle energies beyond the normal physical world. She has travelled widely to research and record the sacred knowledge encoded in ancient places. In her early twenties she was drawn to Mexico and became fascinated by the ancient Mayan healing traditions. There she was trained to use her gift as a seer by an old Mayan healer. She subsequently returned to her native Britain and learned from many other healers and teachers about traditional healing modalities.

While studying the megalithic structures of Britain she saw that undamaged stone circles and menhirs (standing stones) could enhance the natural lines of energy and node points of the Earth, but she also saw that if these nodes and energy lines were blocked and became dark that they could cause illnesses such as cancer or even psychosis in those living nearby. She knew that it was essential to clear these dark lines of force for the health of all people.

Energy lines (sometimes called ley lines) of the Earth are similar in function to the acupuncture meridians on the physical body with specific node points. Gwendolyn found by working with the light from the Source that stagnant or dark energies around people or locations could be removed and balance could be restored.

Using photography, illustration, and the written word, Gwendolyn recorded the unusual events that led up to the summer solstice of 1986 at Callanish. Her description of the inner worlds at work will enthrall the reader and give pause for thought. Gwendolyn sees the Callanish I site like a giant circuit board. Did the megalithic builders really know and understand the methods to enhance life by creating a circuit in stone to harness the dynamic energies of the sun and moon? Did they have an understanding of the DNA five thousand years ago? It appears they may have.

Gwendolyn continues her healing work to help bring balance to people and the Earth and works with clients around the world as a medical intuitive. She is currently based in the USA.

Other books by the author:

The Angels' Guide to Living on Earth published 2002

The Angels' Guide to Forgiveness published 2002

A Cry from the Womb published 2004

The Chalice and the Heart published 2007